Rick —
  Julia & I enjoyed
visit with you. Thanks
for the hospitality!
            Blessings,
            Skip R.
            Sept, 2017

BEARING THE CAST

SAINT JULIAN PRESS

POETRY

PRAISE for BEARING THE CAST

"The word metanoia (typically translated as 'repentance') actually means 'Go into the larger mind.' In that sense, Skip Renker's new collection is a profound act of metanoia; it bears witness to a human being 'caught in the act' of waking up, learning to pay attention from the heart. Clearly detectible beneath the sparse, Zenlike surface of these poems are those deeper shafts of light emerging from a growing compassion, gentleness, and a wry, self-deprecating humor that somehow manages to 'hold all things in unity.'"

The Rev. Cynthia Bourgeault
Episcopal Priest – Writer – Retreat Leader

"In this God-haunted book of poems where the Dhammapada and The Tibetan Book of the Dead seem to exert influence equally with the writings of Thoreau and Meister Eckhart, Skip Renker gives us the world made whole again through a language of remarkable precision and clarity. The old dichotomy of subjective/objective falls away, replaced by the thinking mind bodied forth, which is to say, poetry of a very high order. Bearing the Cast is a magnificent achievement."

B.H. Fairchild – Author
The Blue Buick: New and Selected Poems
National Book Critics Circle Award Winner

"As you read this book, everything around you will grow more vivid. Wherever you live, whatever you see every day—ordinary as it may seem—will snap into a different kind of focus. Skip Renker argues that if we can coax ourselves to be still, if we can look carefully and at length at what lies immediately in our lives, if we can enter silence and pay attention and grasp what we see, we might be transformed. I am grateful for his steadiness, especially during this time of historic upheaval. He is a trustworthy companion. I would follow him anywhere."

Jeanne Murray Walker – Author
Helping the Morning: New and Selected Poems

"It is our good fortune that some books arrive when we need them most. Bearing the Cast, by Skip Renker, is such a book, full of light, tenderness, grace and rich in its observations of the world's natural beauty, making us feel a part of a larger world far beyond the headlines of war, hate, blame, fear. The quiet realm of Skip Renker's poetry helps us see afresh the beauty which surrounds us and quickens our faith. Immerse yourself in Renker's poetry and let your heart be glad again. Hear his self-advice, 'be still for as long as it takes…stand with open palms in an attitude of listening.'"

Jean Connor – Author
A Cartography of Peace and *A Hinge of Joy*

"Skip Renker writes us into his tempestuous love affair with leaves and water and humanity, as if mining the underpinnings of the universe. Inklings of the unseen settle in many of his poetic lines. As he probes mysteries, ironies, ordinaries that prove to be extraordinary his moods move up and down the scale from black humor to jubilation, and in language that justifies it—from 'the plodding ego' to 'bright clarity of appetite.'"

Luci Shaw – Author
Sea Glass: New and Selected Poems
Writer in Residence, Regent College

"This collection bears the imprint, the cast, of devotion to our world, what's seen and unseen. The poems come out of a rich interior life that's working, as it watches a still surface, not anxious for disturbance even as it acknowledges the inevitable. Our attention moves between the river and its banks, flow and stasis, sometimes luring the poet's spirit, sometimes getting the best of his shoes. Skip Renker's literal balance and the good-humored loss of it, memory's agile revisions, the detaching comforts of aging, make this book one to return to, for in its depths, like a river or an attentive mind, it bends, 'looping back' with more to offer as 'its giver, needing nothing, gives and gives.'"

Jeanine Hathaway – Author
Motherhouse; The Self as Constellation; The Ex-Nun Poems

BEARING THE CAST

Poems By

Skip Renker

SAINT JULIAN PRESS
HOUSTON

Published by
SAINT JULIAN PRESS, Inc.
2053 Cortlandt, Suite 200
Houston, Texas 77008

www.saintjulianpress.com

COPYRIGHT © 2017
TWO THOUSAND AND SEVENTEEN
© SKIP RENKER

ISBN-13: 978-0-9986404-2-6
ISBN-10: 0-9986404-2-5
Library of Congress Control Number: 2017935366

Cover Art: *Peacemaker* by Larry Butcher
Author Photo: Michael Jeroragim

For mentors, teachers, and for Julia

CONTENTS

PART 1 THE CAST

SILENT REACH	3
A CORMORANT'S GRIP	4
THE SPEED OF LIGHT	5
SHOES OUTSIDE A DOOR	6
LIGHT MEASURES	7
A HABITABLE SOLSTICE	8
A MOMENTARY OBEDIENCE	10
TEMPLE DIRECTIVE	11
BEARING THE CAST	12

PART 2 APPETITES

IRONY AND ORGASM	17
LEANING ON A WALL	18
GREAT AUNT GERTRUDE'S FIRST WEDDING	20
APPETITES	21
TODAY THE HUMMINGBIRD	23
CANNIBAL CLOWNS STALK DESERT TOWN	24
A GRAVE MAN	26
MEMENTO MORI	28
A GIVING SURFACE	29
A PATH IN THE WOODS	30
TRUTH AND A FRENCH RED	31

PART 3 HONORABLE BEASTS

OWING THE LIGHT	35
LEAVING OFF	36
SNOUT	37
GUESTS AND HOSTS	38
I BOW TO THE RIVER	40
RIVER INVOCATION	42
A FRIENDLY GEOMETRY	44
SURFACE, NOTIONS	45

PART 4 WARY PRAYERS

A PETER LORRE BIOPIC	49
TO A MUSHROOM	51
THE CHEMISTRY OF MELANCHOLY	52
YOUR MONEY	53
THE HEART PATIENT'S INSTRUCTIONS	54
ANESTHESIA	55
AUTUMN SURGERY	57
AFTER AN ILLNESS	58
FROM A RAISED CHAIR	59
ON SLEEPING BEAR DUNES	60
WARY PRAYER	61
A GARBAGE SUTRA	62

PART 5 ABSENCES

TO VIRGINIA WOOLF	67
PRAYER AFTER FINDING AN OLD ADDRESS BOOK	69
SPHERICAL	71
FOR AN UNNAMED FRIEND	72
CONVERTIBLE SUMMER	74
IN THE FEEL	75
I MISSED YOUR FUNERAL	76
AT THE BEDSIDE	77
FROM THE AIRLINER HYMNAL	79
ABSENCES	80

PART 6 LISTENING

REQUEST	85
HIDE AND SEEK	86
ROUGH CIRCLES	87
SKY PRAISES	89
JUGGLER'S HEART	91
A LITTLE NIGHT MUSIC	92
ADMISSIONS	93
SELF ADVICE	94
TO BLESSED MARY	95
DOUBLE EXCAVATION	96
TIME OUT OF TIME	97

ABOUT THE AUTHOR
ACKNOWLEDGEMENTS

> "Deep in their roots,
> All flowers keep the light."
> ~ Theodore Roethke

BEARING THE CAST

PART 1 THE CAST

SILENT REACH

There's a stillness in the world
that lives at dusk in the tapering pines
near the riverbank, light held in high branches,
darkness further down and deeper
in the woods. Nothing is dead,

not the stumps, the trees
bare of leaves, the pine needles
on the forest floor, the smooth rocks parting
the river, and not this stillness,
wholly self-contained,

needing nothing, yet seeming
to wait for us to wake up in it,
as if, like roots, it lives to reach and feed
on the world, to give back through
itself, servant and conduit.

A CORMORANT'S GRIP

The shallow river's surface, almost still,
Blurs images of trees on the bank, where leaves lift
And fall in a mild wind—nothing else to fill
This September day but the mid-river rift

Around a smooth white rock. During a sunny week,
Turtles often warm up there, but today the sure
Grip of a cormorant, green-eyed, black, sleek,
His hook-tipped beak bobbing, as if to conjure

A fish up. Or maybe he's not a bit
Hungry, and such steady small movement
Is play to him, even a way he feeds his spirit,
Or does such instant speculation prevent

My further seeing? The curve of rising wings,
Say, or that other bird in a bankside willow, singing.

THE SPEED OF LIGHT

Once every ten thousand thoughts
Or so, the mind slows,
Lets light in—it might fall
On the birch, leaves

Not yet crisped
By summer heat,
Blue sky darkening
Behind high white branches,

On a bee that zigzags
Among shades of green
Where the arbor vitae
Trembles in the breeze,

And on the motionless car
In the driveway, dusty,
Half in shadow, the cooling
Engine quietly ticking.

SHOES OUTSIDE A DOOR

Drying out, my dunked shoes curl at the toes,
    resembling a pair of stubborn ducks who
        waddle through the world with clipped wings.

Gravity pulled my sneakered feet
    off the bank and down into river mud
        earlier today—nothing personal, just

the law in action as I leaned too far,
    goggling downstream with binoculars
        for the long-eyed heron, stilled fisher

on the far shore. My shoes and my ego
    bathed as he lifted off, bent legs lengthening,
        shedding sunlit water. Was Jesus barefoot

when he walked the sea? Legend
    has it that a school of fish rose
        to ferry him on their backs. Maybe

by then he'd shed his ego, if he ever
    had one, but mine plods along like
        a pair of waterlogged shoes, earthbound,

accident-prone, soaked in itself. Maybe,
    though, the same power that makes the laws
        plants this longing to fly out of our shoes.

We gaze up to interrogate the air,
    then slip them off at the doors of the holy,
        where learning to bow is the first lesson.

LIGHT MEASURES

Pines wheel, rain smacks
    the siding, skylights, deck chairs,
        a wind-chime rings. An afternoon

like this in memory,
    feeling the beginnings of
        wonder—how the dark

massing clouds raced
    the light! A toy truck
        skitters across the sidewalk,

I run in from the yard, soaked,
    my sturdy legs labor up slippery
        wooden steps to the front door,

and my mother enfolds me
    in a bath towel, wipes my arms
        and face, turns me so we look together

toward Little Traverse Bay. Now,
    sixty-some years later—what
        does a year measure? My mother

counts out loud the seconds between
    each clap of thunder, and the delicious
        world makes a new kind of sense.

A HABITABLE SOLSTICE

"The Sagittarius Dwarf, a small galaxy, is colliding with the Milky Way right now." –hubblesite.org

Our planet orbits a serviceable star,
One of billions burning
In this banged-up Milky Way,

While the salmon that leapt upstream
Sizzles on the backyard grill, and wine
That began as grapes on a Tuscan hillside
Chills in a bucket of melting ice.

My friend leans forward in her lawn chair
To caution Justin, who rides
His first two-wheeler under apple trees

Flanking the patio, their brown-edged
Leaves, even on this first day
Of summer, already shredded
By insects. The world's a scary place

For kids these days, she tells me,
But the boy pedals hard in widening circles,
Just slow enough not to topple off

Onto this generous planet, giving its all
In a tough galactic neighborhood.
"Be careful!" she calls. Justin, though,

Won't stop to sit under an apple tree
And wait for fruit to ripen and fall—
Immersed in the laws of gravity
And acceleration, lungs nearly bursting,

The wind rippling leaves and his shirttails,
He steers with one tightly gripping hand,
Waves with the other.

A MOMENTARY OBEDIENCE

How the laws must love us, my sweet—
Gravity, thermodynamics, whatever
Makes sunlight slant and creates
The splayed shadow of an aging oak,
This exact, never-to-be-repeated
Invitation to come out of the heat,
To look up through sober obedient
Branches, their leaves, I like to think,
Pleased by the wind, and a blue swath of sky
Sentient as you or me. The implacable

Laws love one another, too—
No light without weight, no movement
Without time. Though we will succumb
To the brutality of accident, or
To cancer, weakened hearts, even
Inner demons obeying the dictates
Of their natures, right now there's this
Never-to-be-repeated moment,
So let us, love, lie down on the grass
In the cool shade of its mercy.

TEMPLE DIRECTIVE

Know the klickklack bird,
Nester in temples, wings
Of the upper reaches. Happy
Its song, the silence
Between notes, and the man
Who sees in blue, man of rafters,
Of domes open to the sky.
Know the woman of levels,
Elevators, unseen ladders,
Bright stars. Know the temple
Of fulfillment, happy
Its mandalas of light.

Know too the temple
Of shadows, the passage
From light to darkness—know
All modulation. Know
The beggars in the temple
Streets, the arthritic, the starving,
The limbless, the heart
In its disease. Know the rifle,
The bayonet, the missile, the bomb.
Know consciousness
And the unconscious.
Know enigma. Know

The klickklack bird,
The wind, the dust, the straw,
The woven nest.

BEARING THE CAST

"For God's love is very like a fishhook."
—Meister Eckhart

On the upper reaches of the Manistee
Or another trout stream, a flash
Of silver catches your eye—

Flick of the wrist toward the leaf-shadowed
Feeder in the shallows, leader line
Whistling past your ear,

And the hook rides along ripples, its
Barb hiding in the hackle of a fly,
Impeccably tied iridescence.

You know, it seems, that we
Can't bear the sight of love
Undisguised on the waters,

How the beauty that hides
The iron in your desire
Lures us to rise,

Lunge, swallow, writhe,
How the sleek, scaly,
Ravenous parts of our being

Must die before
We learn to live
Within your tendered cast.

PART 2 APPETITES

IRONY AND ORGASM

You call for action, but your
Private parts are lazing about
Again, prima donnas who refuse
To take the stage, would-be stars
Who just won't shoot for the moon,

But if the principle of creation
Is both male and female, then
Orgasms keep making this world
Of pheromones, foreskins, aureoles,
Desire, love, and of course
Irony, which never makes anything,

So while you hover above the bed,
Your lover, yourself, astral backside
Bumping the ceiling, you might think
How ironists—the critic, the comedian,
The wise-cracking wallflower—all have their
Places in the great scheme of things,

Which includes supple porn stars,
Doomed lovers, saints pierced by
The white-hot swords of angels,
And how passion comes eventually
In one of its infinite forms, or none of us

Would be here, comes up from your
Heels, zips down from the ceiling
Or heaven, comes so you can
Give yourself away again, and give
The mind, sooner or later,
Something to stand back from.

LEANING ON A WALL

On constant alert, how much
My penis meant to me at fifteen,
No less on a quest than Gawain
Or Lancelot, no less base or holy
In its instincts. Now in my sixties
My left hand holds it while my right
Presses on the bathroom wall between
Two prints, one of dormant Mt. Fuji,
The other of a lily leaning tentatively
Toward the light, but that teenager
Lives on in me, ghostly, astral,
Reaches with the same arm,
Same hand. He hoped
That by acting sullen or appearing
Politely opaque, he could hide
His interior, error-prone knight
From the adults in his world,
Not yet realizing there's more
To life than its private parts,
And that for all their talk
Even those four or five times
Older were still being schooled—
Maybe always would be—
In that perilous discipline,
The alchemy of love. He
And his penis still had to learn,
Mostly the hard way, that you're
On your own when it comes
To mixing the ingredients—

There's no Merlin to stir
The cauldron, serve up the saving
Potion, and no Zen or other master
To put an arm around you,
Point a finger at the moon.

GREAT AUNT GERTRUDE'S FIRST WEDDING

Under the lights of the Big Top, Gert fell
For the inked designs on the acrobat's chest.
"I loved the way the cobra spiraled
When he flexed his muscles,"
She told us. Mesmerized, she watched him
Perform handstands on the wide seat
Of his gleaming motorcycle, or somersault
In and out of the chrome-plated sidecar.
Then he'd don his leather jacket and goggles,
Take her for a ride.

On the morning of the wedding, eyeing
Her swelling belly and the long train
Of her gown in the full-length mirror,
Gert wobbled like a tentpole in a high wind.
"Mother, even when he's lifting weights
Or showing me how to swab the stuff
That makes his chest glisten, he never
Stops picking at what I say, the way I dress,
Everything. I love him, but it hurts."
Gert's widowed mother bit down on two pins,
Flicked a thread off the dress. "Patience
Is as patience does. You made your bed,
Sweetie. Now you have to lie in it."

When the minister cleared his throat
After the question, Gert almost said "Tattoo,"
Then twined her arms around the torso
Of her husband, kissed him
Like there was no tomorrow.

APPETITES

Pigs squeal, stuck with the rest of us
In a Detroit traffic jam, waves
Of August heat mingling with exhaust fumes
And the odor from a twelve-wheeler
With block letters on the driver's door:
Bad Axe Hogs—Best in Michigan's Thumb,
And I'm back up there in the Sixties,

Where my best friend married
A pig farmer's daughter. She kicked off
Her pumps, revealing the delicate arch
Of her instep, while grunts and squealing
From the pole barn competed
With the polka band, most of us drunks
Dancing on the mowed square near the ripe
Squash and melons filling the garden.
A sow roasted on the backyard spit, slowly
Revolving with a Jonathan apple in its mouth.

"She's good enough to eat," the groom sighed,
Gazing at his bride in her off-the-shoulder taffeta,
Swapping insider Polish jokes with his great uncle,
Who'd come over from Warsaw to cook
For northern logging camps in a nation
With an unappeasable appetite for
Michigan's virgin trees—oak, maple, hemlock,
Pines two-hundred feet tall hewed down
For the furniture factories of Grand Rapids,
Millworkers' row houses in the East,
The mansions of Newport. I pull even

With the pigs. Some bump and jostle
At the center of the flatbed, as if
In a hurry to die and bleed
On the slaughterhouse floor, or conspiring
To bust out, run broken-field like halfbacks
Through stalled traffic to the nearest forest.
I could reach over, place a palm on a forehead.

Hair grows in random clumps on the snout
That pokes through wooden slats, lifts
And twitches. Pink-rimmed eyes rove,
Then focus, curious as a human's.

TODAY THE HUMMINGBIRD

Hovers, abuzz with bewilderment,
Veers this way and that—
The apparently unseen flowers
Three feet below could be
Thirsty too for the thirsty bird,
Who looks momentarily
At me--my head, my hair
Might be bougainvillea—

Then light darts across his brain,
And he dives for petals
And nectar, his divining rod
Trembling with precision,
And I long on this day
In which I've been lost
In mists, miles from purpose,
For the bright clarity of appetite.

CANNIBAL CLOWNS STALK DESERT TOWN
—for Helen Ruggieri

After another insomniac night,
I roll over at 6:30 A.M., click
The remote. Giant clowns exit
Two flying saucers, wield aerosol cans
The size of oil barrels while they roam
Main Street in a high desert town.
They spray its citizens pink
And green, create a sticky shroud
Like cotton candy; then the lengthy
Tongues of the alien bozos
Lick people to death, long spirals
Of ecstasy for both victim
And predator that terminate
In a fully satisfied mutual sigh,
So powerful it blows needles off
The cacti. Lord, it's tempting

To sweeten and fatten, to be iced,
To freeze up until you're a Sno-Cone,
Consenting fully, at last, to becoming
Dessert for a ravenous universe
In a life that so often seems
One long joke with infinite variations
On comic swoons and dying falls—
To die, to be dead to the world, in
On the punchline at last. But Lord

Krishna in the Gita, no comedian,
Scares me as he scared Arjuna, projecting
The vision of multi-headed, fiery-mouthed
Shiva, his many arms stuffing the recently
Dead left and right down his gullets.
His message to the warrior, who wanted
To lie down and die rather than fight:
"You better wake up, buddy, or this
Is where your afterlife is headed."

Leaning over the sink, for a moment
I gaze with longing at the running water,
Wishing it were the River Lethe, then
I remind myself that Arjuna went back
To work after his hair stopped standing
On end. I splash my face, slap it
Left and right with the rough affection
Oliver Hardy showed the equally
Foolish Laurel, both reeling but still
Upright after the Sisyphean labor
Of pushing and hauling the piano
Up the wide outdoor stairway, then
Slippage, the slow-gathering backslide,
The tinkling keys, the cacophonous
Descent. Better awake and smiling,
Even forcing a laugh, I tell myself,
Than crushed by a runaway Steinway,
Or eaten up from within or without.

–based on the movie title,
Killer Klowns from Outer Space

A GRAVE MAN

It's alive! I hear myself say,
Six days into Spring,
The first redwing blackbirds
Scrawing from last year's cattails,
Ditchwater sluicing through mushy ice.
The monster's awake, and I could
Dance an electrified two-step,
Jive like my friend who imitated
Wild-eyed Dr. Frankenstein, body
Quivering as if wired, voice
Shuddering through *alive!*

Michael found the joke in almost
Everything, but he couldn't kid
About the bag his surgeons
Installed, until he rallied
Shortly before he died, punning
On colostomy, *Losta my all*,
In Chico Marx Italian.

It's alive, but you're not,
Michael, at least not
In these parts. I dream
That we dangle our feet
From a long dock, looking
Toward dark water,
And the creature from the black lagoon
Slowly rises—scaly, slimy,
With one large misshapen eye,
A monster with a gaze we return
In silence for an unbearable
Number of beats before you
Deliver one of your deadpan lines.

MEMENTO MORI

The stinking vulture perched
On the ribcage of the dead deer
Is hard to love, his jackhammer
Head and neck plunging again and again
Into muscle, tendons, gristle,
Marrow, his needy appetites
So undisguised. There's no

Cruelty or greed in him, though,
And he's not a grave-robbing
Ghoul—hunger appeased,
He quits eating. Unlike
Dr. Frankenstein, he hunts by day,
Lives by the laws, and would never
Dream of reconstruction. He neither
Murders nor creates. Sometimes

He circles slowly, seemingly
Just for the hell of it, swerves
And dips into graceful spirals,
Plays with the currents, as if
A winged body could savor
Flight alone, forgetting for awhile
How much its hunger needs the dead.

A GIVING SURFACE

After thunder, rain, the swollen river,
    a sluggish stink-bug with a missing
feeler's baffled by the window surface—
    five appendages and two antennae
probe, twitch, a world of green in sunset light
    an eighth-of-an-inch away.

I cup the creature,
    release it out the door, a moment
in two lives. My big brain's teeming,
    but with what? Occasional compassion,
rare clarity, but more often an unconscious
    proliferation of fog-thick thought
that misses sunlight on a blue chairback,
    grass underfoot, a friend's needful heart.
I'm far from what's right in front of me.

    Today as I watched a doe drink
from the shallows, lift and plant her forelegs
    in a slow dance of power and delicacy,
I wished to return as one of her kind,
    even to endure the frequent, sudden fears,
autumn rifles, frost, snow, parasites, seasons
    of dull hunger, just to move with that same
jointed rise and fall, run if I must or wanted to,
    haunches rippling, all four legs and hooves
moving, sensing, in direct contact
    with the given, surface of the earth.

A PATH IN THE WOODS

Don't seek the odor
    of sanctity, some ecstatic saints
say, but cultivate instead
    the sense that leads
to spiritual thirst. They record
    an aroma, only half-otherworldly,
neither honey-sweet nor quite
    like sourmash—sniff,
and your nerve endings bristle,
    send it mile after labyrinthine mile
down through memory and beyond.

Discern the odor's slow modulation
    from grass clippings to diesel fuel
to fresh flyblown dung,
    dried up spiders in basement corners,
grandmother's rose water, a sunflower
    you stuck your nose in at four.

The saints tell us to stay on the scent,
    which will lead your horse
through a forest to a clear pool
    where it may or may not, depending
on grace and your training, your touch
    with reins and bridle, stretch
its beautiful neck and head to drink.

TRUTH AND A FRENCH RED
"Drink not the third glass, which thou canst not tame."
—George Herbert, *"The Church Porch"*

Too much equals befuddlement,
But not enough leaves the autocratic
Brain in command. So two glasses
Of vino, just the right *veritas*—

I drink to the hair that silkens her forearms!
I drink to nimble fingers twirling stemware!
I drink to the lift in her thighs!
Lobes in temporary harmony, my brain

Rises to our occasion, sun-facing hillsides
Of skin, tender bones, serpentine twining
And all the rest, then the sober familiar
Returning: tristesse, ennui, trip

To the bathroom, don faded once-red robe
And post-coital mental blah-blah re:
Sex as the little dying, Wallace Stevens
On death as the mother of beauty,

Or maybe mother of nothing at all,
Dust to dust, etc. So what? Love is
Still in the *veritas* of uncorked bottles,
Her slowed breathing and sleepy eyelids,
Our bodies, this momentary air.

PART 3 HONORABLE BEASTS

OWING THE LIGHT

Up to a few million years ago,
No humans existed, no human eye beheld
The glow of autumn sumac at sunset,
The rippled brightness of yellowing elms.

The optic nerves of a grazing mastodon
Must've registered photonic nuances beyond
The power of hunters, but our ancestors still
Saw enough in Pleistocene dusk to kill, eat,

Clothe themselves in its hide. Fullness, warmth,
And four hundred generations or so
Led to the leisure I savor this evening
Under off-white clouds and darkening blue—

What a wonder to stand outside on a world
That sifted fallen flesh, organs, bones,
Slowly pulverized or burned them to ash;
All molecular now, yet somehow

Still present. I owe the beast everything,
The hunters and gatherers, owe the maker-evolver
Of the eye, owe for the luck I feel dawning
In my body, owe Orion, owe the Pleiades.

LEAVING OFF

To leave off everything but looking
At my neighbor's chestnut mare, out
Beyond the fence in this twilight—
She may be looking back—I see
Her dark flanks, her large white

Forehead star. To leave the remembered
Quarrel, this lingering soreness
Around my heart, the grey shroud
I walked around in all day, to look
Up at the reddish billowing

Of the slow-moving clouds, the sea-like
Sky, to smell the air, the northwest wind
Playing around my ankles, the grass
Under my soles cushioning
The firm earth. To leave off

Everything but looking, breathing,
Rocking a little from side to side,
Forward and back, and to listen, to hear
The mare neigh, softly, twice,
As she canters along the fenceline.

SNOUT

To be something like
An aardvark. To possess
A black sniffer, moist, the
Insides of broad nostrils
Lined with veins that wind
Like crimson snakes far back
Into the brain. To slaver
Above stiff whiskers that taper,
And thick red fur, matted
Around lips curving like pink
Sickle moons. To draw them back
For small white teeth, rounded nubs
In blue-black gums. To inhale,
Snuffle dirt, insects, every
Grub and worm in your path,
To eat your fill and shuffle off
To a deep den. Heavy-lidded,
To roll sideways, to welcome
The muzzle of sleep.

GUESTS AND HOSTS

I wake to stars and the dim bulb
    of the moth-battered streetlight,
while microbial mites, invisible

to my wide-open insomniac eyes, scurry
    over sheets and bedding, trek
across the hills and valleys of my body—

ids incarnate on microscope slides,
    insectisoid monsters, Sci-Fi fodder,
but in this living host they're driven

by hunger to navigate ear canals,
    swim through tear ducts,
slip through the borders of the brain.

In sated moments, maybe they pause,
    take in lightning storms—ignited
neurons—and tilt antennae for rumbles

of thunder from the thinker
    they inhabit, who watches the moths,
wonders if the spheres really

make music, and whether light
    can be fully explained by mathematics
and telescopic investigation. Surely

light's alive, more like a being
    who singes if instinct leads to foolish
diving, but if you keep a respectful

distance, greets you with welcoming eyes
    at the entrance, ushers you in
to the electrifying party.

I BOW TO THE RIVER

To the 10,000 raindrops
That pockmark its surface
And to the overarching wings
Of the waterfowl-god, progenitor
Of mallards and mergansers,
Who sculpts the heron's
S-curved neck, sends forth
The osprey and the eagle.

Though toxins leach in from
Upstream factories and farms,
The river still reflects the first
Yellow in the poplars, reveals
Among the shadows of floating leaves
Dark, bottom-feeding fish,
While shy deer pick their way
Down slippery banks to drink.

In my own darker moments
I fear that our mammalian brains,
Given over to the bottom-feeding
Gods of chance and expedience,
Will continue to fail the rain
And the light at the headwaters,

But it's still pouring and for now
Mud at the edges of the banks
Has a certain slurred beauty,
And the roots of cedars grope,
Millimeter by millimeter,
Like a half-blind hope beneath the wind,
And the kingfisher rises and dips,
Dips and rises, upstream and down.

RIVER INVOCATION

My river's no Tigris or Euphrates,
No Nile—it's never meandered
Through numbered dynasties—
I have only these thickly wooded banks
And this muddy flow called The Pine,
Where the first mallards of spring
Fly upstream, and buffleheads

Dip for minnows. Some brains
Know just enough to drive a beak
Into prey, swallow, digest,
While bigger brains sculpt the face
Of a pharaoh on the body of a lion,
Human brains that started growing
Way back before the Paleolithic,
So bring on the river cultures, I say,

As well as Shiva dancing
The headwaters of the Ganges
Into being, and the guardian
Archangel of the Mississippi
Who works ceaselessly to save it,
And bring on all souls
Migrating in the Boat of Ra,
And bring on too the unseen

Builder of the ferry to the far shore,
Effortless wielder of neutrinos,
Electrons, quarks and the laws,
And bring it all back home to this earth,
To the baby Moses alone and crying
In the bulrushes, to the deer
That drink from my Pine, to trout
Rising, to the beaver and the otter.

A FRIENDLY GEOMETRY

Because the pines that climb the banks
    achieve today this exact tapered height,
        and the November sky cleared overnight,
I stand outside instead of in, stunned
    by shafts of slanted light, mid-woods,
        and over the river, fifty-foot
parallelograms drifted with rising mist.

Now and then such friendly intersections
    of law and human love, lucky effects
        of the light, I think to myself,
tilting the bill of my cap to shade
    but not completely block
        the water's rippling shine.

Transparent leaves angle across my vision,
    and I'm here for the heron, who lifts
        after dipping for fish beyond the cattails,
herky-jerky legs and misted wings dangling,
    all ungainly until beak, head, and neck
        align like an arrow, feathered and aimed
upstream at the sun's risen disc.

SURFACE, NOTIONS

The riverside maple lives out
From its invisible core, moist
Rings, serrated bark. Halfway up
The trunk, a harnessed man leans away,
Sings while he prunes
With long-handled clippers,
Hums for the delicate trimming,
Then goes full-throated again, as if
Giving voice to the mute tree,
The meaning of its life and the ways
It draws moisture up from roots and out
To leaves on a windless spring day.

Mergansers, red-billed, white-backed
Navigators of air and water, dive
For minnows and crawdads, swim
Twenty yards underwater, surface
With a flutter, launch into flight—
They inhabit one element, feed
In another, like certain graced notions
That rise into consciousness,
Then disappear again, or so a man
Who climbed a tree might think
As he drives the pickup home, drums
On the dashboard to radio music,

The bright river winding through shadows
Of spruce, cedar, maple, oak.

PART 4 WARY PRAYERS

A PETER LORRE BIOPIC

A boy fleeing a pogrom—
I was born Laszlo Lowenstein—
I sought out fetid pits and brush-covered
Depressions, fascinated by five-hearted
Night crawlers, their segments going separate
Ways to worm slow motion into the dampness
Of the European earth. Soon enough,

The continent ripped itself apart—
By then I'd learned to emote from that cellar
In myself where the dream intruder
Drags a casket over the echoing
Stone floor. The Nazis who specialized
In maggots, the swarming life of corpses,
Drove Brecht, von Stroheim, Wilder,
And me from Berlin—I escaped into

The grand illusion of American movies,
Kingdom of the ersatz, good glorified,
Bad smashed, thank you, Mr. Moto.
I swallowed arsenic in the blackest
Of comedies, outwitted by two-faced crones,
My last words as seductive and insinuating
As our temptation to the death wish. Even
The child I murdered in M wanted it
A little. Sometimes I invited Brecht,
My Red friend, to watch the rough cuts,
Just to make the Hollywood moguls squirm.
We too despise McCarthy, they'd say, but—

There's the only history lesson
You need—always a <u>but</u>. Still,
Watching my rushes I had moments
During close-ups of frightened eyes,
Moist, soulful, globular, when even
I felt strangely sympathetic
To that evil, vulnerable creature
Acting from the gnome-like body
Which guarded, as if it were deep
Beneath the screen, such dark treasure.

TO A MUSHROOM

Rain-generated,
Fungoid, white-domed,
You didn't choose
This beautiful
Slant of sunlight
Across your bald head,
Which rises like a lord's
Over the storm-beaten
Grasses. You must be

Unconscious, like
And unlike the human
Brain you resemble,
With its primitive
Stem and evolved
Neocortex that together
Procreated the Bomb,
Named its poison
Cloud after you.

THE CHEMISTRY OF MELANCHOLY

Is there not something sad
About the ingredients of our shampoos,
About cetearyl alcohol and the way it blends
With behentrimonium chloride?
Perhaps in this or a parallel
Universe there's joy in such merging,
Yet I can't help feeling melancholy
For propylene glycol, dimethiconol,
And an even deeper sadness
For all the numbered experiments
With form and function that led
To the solution of quaternium-91.

Driving home to their families,
Do the blenders and labelers
Ever feel they've lost their real names,
Become Ms. Utica Dioica or Mr. Panthenol?
Do they transmit their heritage
To the children—sweet Hexyl Cinnamic,
Or wistful Chamomilla, brushing
For hours in front of the mirror?

So much effort to feed our hair
Castor oil/sebacic acid co-polymer,
Not to mention equisetum/horsetail;
So much cutting and plucking
In corrals and labs, so many
Test tubes, so much conditioning,
So many eyes filling with sodium chloride,
Salty tears spilling down cheeks.

YOUR MONEY

How it longs to be
Anything else—
Burritos, lasagna,
A bag of nectarines,
Boxes of handmade
Panatelas, a gem
Or fifty convertibles.

If you hoard,
It weasels out of
Safes and shoeboxes
Right after your funeral,
And deadbeat relatives
With twitchy fingers
Leap to satisfy
Its urge to be liquid
Or solid—a lakefront home,
Or a gleaming 4-by-4
With Hydrodrive
And custom flames
Painted on the fenders.

Always itching
For the ecstasies
Of conversion,
It's as American
As pulling up stakes.
It has no self-esteem,
And only one demand:
Give me a makeover
.

THE HEART PATIENT'S INSTRUCTIONS

If I should tumble
From the gurney, leave me
In a heap. Let doctors step
Around me with care, aides
And nurses provide a wide berth.
Delay the ether, the gas,
The injection—whatever
Might be waiting to ease me
Toward the knife. Let me be—
I ask only for a decent interval—
Like a still life. Give me
The floor, no matter how
Hard, scuffed, or dirty,
And the annoying, reassuring
Hum of fluorescent tubes,
The scratch and rustle
Of white starched clothing,
The ordinary, irregular
Beat of rubber-soled shoes
.

ANESTHESIA

As he slides under, his body
Goes limp beneath the sheet,
His right hand prescribes
A lazy arc, flops against the edge
Of the operating table. It's
Ready to reach for something
"Scrumptious," a word
That floats on the surface
Of his mind, like a toy boat
Seen from below in a swimming pool,
A word his mother loved to use,
Offering a sweet when he'd eaten
All his supper. He smells rancid
Chocolate. There are wheels, gears
Clanking inside and below him,
And a parade of animals—
Palominos, German Shepherds,
Two giraffes, and some creature
That slithers around the ankles
Of an orderly. A doctor

Dressed in white, wearing
A brown woolen hood, lifts off
From a corner of his childhood
Bedroom, flying like Dumbo
Across the ceiling, his trunk
And a curlicue of tail
Shadowed by the nightlight,
The shadow lengthening as he

Descends, something shiny
And sharp between his thumb
And the first two fingers
Of his gloved hand.

AUTUMN SURGERY

You'll likely see seventy and beyond,
The turning of more seasons than most
Of your ancestors, because synaptic
Sparks fired up an inventor's brain

In the technological heart, not entirely dark,
Of the Twentieth Century. Now tunnel-tubes
Brace artery walls—you're a product
Of history with history's product
Nestled in your chest. In this

Irreplaceable moment of slimmed-down
Evening light, your hand rises of its own
Accord at your bedroom window, a gesture
You recognize as comically apt,
To your robed heart, and you watch grandchildren

Through sudden tears. The boy scoops and flings
Piles of yellow-brown leaves, two-handed,
At his older sister, who ignores him
With a startling purity of intention
While turning cartwheel after cartwheel.

AFTER AN ILLNESS

I almost inhabit the old me—
I reach for steering wheel and keyboard,
Fret, launch the familiar schemes,
My cough at last an irregular
Visitor, not the boarder who muscled in
For a week. I no longer

Groan when limbs lift and turn,
But I'm half-nostalgic
For that figure lying on the bed
Who dozed or fever-dreamed through
Chills and sweats. He seems now
Like a faintly remembered god,

His only calendar the sharp-edged,
Slow-moving shadows from a painful sun,
His moons evolving through eons—
He put off everything, predicted nothing,
And lived, though barely, without
Pleasure and without a qualm.

FROM A RAISED CHAIR

Above shelves of Vitalis, Wildroot,
Colored gels and combs, an 1899
Photograph of loggers in winter camp, posed
Stiffly with axes and a man-length saw,
Matted locks pushed under caps or tumbling
Over the collar of a mackinaw.
Their wives and lovers collected snippets
For felt-lined boxes, braided tresses,
Listened to cream-oiled quartets who
Maybe minister now when Jehovah,
Bare feet pillowed on a cloudtop,
Calls for brush and clippers. We men

In elevated chairs don't hang our soles
Over the firmament. One barber
Pokes a broom under our shoes, sweeps
Hair across scuffed linoleum—my grey,
The rotund salesman's wispy brown,
And white from quiet, baggy-eyed Walter,
Whose wife died last spring. We leave
Such passings unsung, talk weather
And sports, though from this human height
I think of the penitent woman who
Dried Christ's feet with her hip-length hair,
Threw her life into God's, invented
A language of kisses and weeping.

ON SLEEPING BEAR DUNES

A large moth crawls along the beach, its antennae
    Twitching, one wing broken across the middle
        Like a gale-toppled sail. It straggles

To a stop, body grey as stones I skip with you,
    For whom every gnarled root and trout entrail
        Speaks—there are no accidents, you often say.

I wonder where you get such assurance, while
    I'm static-ridden, a component missing, often
        Too close or too far from the signal.

The starving she-bear hunkered down,
    Scanned the wave-lashed lake for her children,
        Unwilling to admit they'd drowned, but you

Love the legend's ending, The Great Spirit
    Sculpting dunes from the mother's body, raising
        The Manitou Islands in the shape of her cubs—

You're attuned to a frequency where suffering
    Is always transmuted, ancestral bears become
        Immortals. The moth drags itself over

A sandy ridge, soon dead in this and all worlds, I say,
    Trying, as usual, for the last word, but you raise
        An eyebrow, tilt your head toward the Islands.

WARY PRAYER

Little more than a fleck
Of orange, an insect wobbles
Across the worn blue carpet
Where communicants will soon
Be walking. Above us,
A steeple, shafts of stained light,
Dust motes, but I see no other
Of the ladybug's number.
When I look again, she flies
A slow zigzag, guided imperfectly
By God knows what—
Hunger? Pheromones?—
Past our Madonna of the hooded eyes
And welcoming palms, the priest
In the bright plumage
Of the season's vestments.
She's a mortal emissary
From the unimaginable Intelligence
That numbers our every hair,
Knows the meaning and whereabouts
Of the white-throated sparrow,
The field, the savannah, the song
And the vesper. Or she's a flicker
Of life in a lawful vastness
That seems random in all
Its effects, and who cares
If one human notices?
With a wary prayer, I too rise
And move forward toward the host.

A GARBAGE SUTRA
"All that we are is the result of what we have thought."
—*The Dhammapada*

Winter boots crunching ice, I wheel garbage
Over snow-packed driveway humps,

Wondering if I scrunched the twist-tied
Tall kitchen bag deep enough, or if seams

Might split, splatter the used-up, the cast off,
The sticky, the stinking. Product engineers

Spend their lives in well-heated labs
Dreaming this stuff up—how to machine

Plastic, tint glass, toast a million
Wheat Chex without burning even one.

My stiffened gloved fingers are freezing,
But I slow down, watch where I'm going,

Get a grip. I don't want to slip, fall,
Bang my head. Bleeding, my last thoughts

Might be about garbage—I could tumble down
The cosmic chute into the garbage bardo.

The Tibetan Book of the Dead says
Your body drops away like a useless bag,

But that other you is a dense cloud
Of thoughts drifting into the next realm.

When I must fall, let me think beyond
The coffin made by my loyal friend,

An artist with wood, who will help my wife
And children slide it lovingly onto the ferry,

The river warm and wide, a sweet-smelling
Wind ruffling palm trees on the far shore.

PART 5 ABSENCES

TO VIRGINIA WOOLF

I'm reading how your natural world
Turned malignant, how you succumbed
To fear-inducing tendrils of vine and weed,
Your mind after years of such attacks
At last giving way to the river,
To the weight of rocks loaded
In voluminous pockets. My own

River, forty yards off,
Sent this dragonfly, which alights
On my forearm, side-mounted
Eyes impersonal and voracious.
I blow the spindly four-winged
Insect off my arm, and I hear
A crop duster over farmers' fields,
Spraying insecticide, and gaze
At your long grave face, strong jaw,
Beautiful eyes, the right slightly askew
In the dust jacket photograph. The law
Pulled you under, the same gravity

Wilbur and Orville Wright dared
And revered, studying flight patterns
And bird anatomy, making aeroplanes
From chicken wire and bicycle parts.
You were twenty-one when they
Lifted off the dunes at Kitty Hawk—
Death-flirts, half-suicidal, they knew how
To suppress, as if their sanity depended on it,
The frightful image of the downward spiral.

Bass rise to feed, a few clouds drift over,
Seventy or more years after you waded in
And sank. Some sages—you must have
Read this, too, or heard it in London
From an itinerant swami—say the mind
Can become like the sky, reflecting
The benign source that gives rise to the stream
Of consciousness. Did death make you wiser?
I ask as if you hear me, while I watch
This hummingbird that hovers
In iridescent suspension between the sky
And the bougainvillea, neither up
Nor down, sane nor insane, mutually
Supported by air and the effort of wings.

PRAYER AFTER FINDING AN OLD ADDRESS BOOK

Many of these old friends
Must have forgotten me, too,
Our recollections not so much
Erased as sunken, galleons
That foundered, drifted down
Through the dark to the ocean floor.

I've heard that in the moment of death
You project something like a movie,
An unflinching, brightly-lit replay
That reveals our life, frame by frame,
Yet flashes past in an instant. If this
Film manifests one of your
Inescapable laws, so be it.
But may I remind you
That I've grown dim-eyed
From seeing the world, far too often,
In monochrome grey--I don't believe
I'll be ready for your bright clarity.
So forgive me—I'm asking
For a longer reckoning.

Give me things tangible,
A diver's suit, an oxygen tank,
A waterproof lamp. I'll descend
To a jumble of splintered beams
And cockeyed portholes,
Captain's wheel and barrel staves,
A chest spilling out handfuls of coins
Stamped with the faces of old friends.
I'll surface to clean and polish, while
You bring them to mind again,
Clearly, one by one
In the slow-gathering light of dawn.

SPHERICAL

When you catch
    the reflection of distant grass
        in a drifting bubble, blown

say, by a grandchild,
    the grass slants, as if
        it wants to lie down

among friends. A bubble
    will play if you touch it
        the way another bubble

might, lightly. No bubble
    is lasting, though some float
        for years, even centuries,

in photographs and paintings—we gaze,
    lost in the visual music of spheres,
        as if our leisure might go on forever.

FOR AN UNNAMED FRIEND

What do I call you, unsigned painter
    of "Distant Trees," beautifully shaped
        swatches rising into a halo of sky

and spilling over hills? Wherever
    you are, my friend, your eyes are darker
        than the rain-wet trunks of oaks in the yard

beyond the window. Where, though,
    is your name? A gust shook loose
        thirty or more leaves all at once

from the poplar across the river—
    they drifted down in patterns,
        taking my breath away. That

was yesterday, when I knew
    your name. It's more meaningful
        than ninety-nine I remember.

Can I not conjure it the way
    I conjure you so easily,
        large strong features, black

eyebrows, your competent hands?
    You're painted in my mind,
        lively and concrete, but your name's

gone beyond abstract, disappeared
    like one of those notes John Cage
        thought up but left out. Is it

skittering over water, has it sunk
    to the bottom, its yellow shine
        darkened to brown? Does it even

matter that I've lost it,
    as I'm losing others I've loved,
        and sometime, sooner or later,

the pictures will go too, the mind,
    the brain, the body? I feel
        more alive with you—our best

moments find a form, a shape
    that suits us both. Maybe enough,
        for now, just to call you friend.

CONVERTIBLE SUMMER

Freshly cut grass blew into my Impala,
A leaf or two, those seedpod whirlybirds.
Like a rajah in a sedan chair, I honked
At friends along the sidewalks
Of our three-block Main Street,
Permitted glimpses of my imperial,
Playful hand. The wind was everything

On the back roads, my girl and I
Absurdly happy with the flesh
Pressing our cheekbones, my arm around
Her bare tanned shoulders, northern Michigan
Hills rolling under us, sunlight
Flashing through trees. So memory,

Ceaseless sifter, never settling
For ungilded being, excises
Tiffs, repairs, the rainy spell in July,
Adds the chrome, polishes the silver
Tailpipe, invents the detailing,
Customizes that ragtop summer.

IN THE FEEL

My father's long fingers, free
Of arthritis even in old age,
Tapered to immaculate nails,
A manicure his bi-weekly
Indulgence. He'd flirt
Gravely while young hands
Lifted and buffed. His
Had a life of their own
With racquets and golf clubs—
"It's all in the feel," he'd say
After an ace or the sinking
Of a twenty-foot putt. Flirting
Was the first of myriad moves
That led to this hour on a porch
In Michigan, the hand I observe
By moonlight, father's and mother's,
Mine and not mine. It seems,
When I'm a little drunk,
Like a brainy cousin, friendly
But remote. A palmist read
The long lifeline years ago—
Flesh, blood, bones, knit in
A mystery I wanted revealed,
But I've forgotten everything
She said. So much of us disappears,
Ice floes in a spring river,
But here I am for the moment,
Reaching for the photograph
Of my sons playing catch
Next to the redbud, its tangle
Of branches, new leaves
Sprouting from the tips.

I MISSED YOUR FUNERAL

Instead, I sat on the porch steps you repaired
And painted, Bill, remembering your competence
With T-Square and chainsaw, the cleared
Riverbank, your wry wit, how you talked sense.

The only time I ever saw you at a loss
Was the day you brought up the prognosis,
Your clear-eyed, open face crisscrossed
With worry lines. Thanks for telling us,

I said—such inadequate words!--and I shook
Your hand. Now you've shed the scaffolding,
Shuffled off to Buffalo, and as I look
Around our house, I'm hoping you died feeling

At home with yourself. Here where you helped us
Live, the kitchen shelves hold firm, the windows
You fitted stay snug, and this cold night
We'll burn the logs you helped haul and split.

AT THE BEDSIDE

I found my bald friend's head all but
Irresistible, and settled my hand on it,
A liberty I'd not have taken if he'd been
Conscious, the everyday Jerry. But where

Else is a hand to find rest under harsh
Fluorescence, multiple tubes and monitors,
The brutal but necessary machines?
He couldn't respond to my voice

Or see me gesture, and his own hands
Twitched, trembled, small immeasurable
Earthquakes beneath the sheet. My thumbnail
Edged his monkish fringe of hair,

And my eyes closed of their own accord,
As if to give the fingertips free rein
To read the contours of my friend's
Head, a relief map of low hills

He often raised his own hands to,
Rubbing it like a crystal ball, exclaiming
"Jesus!" or "Oh, Brother!" when life,
As it often did, both exasperated

And amused him. For a moment,
As my palm relaxed, his pate
Felt cool, a kind of oasis,
And I remembered the childhood

Obsession he told me about,
Building model destroyers, PT boats,
Aircraft carriers, working alone
In his room for months, creating

His own private water-based world
In dry, landlocked Amarillo, and later
His tales of escape from the abusive
Older brother, hellfire preacher uncles,

A shades-down home life that suffocated.
No wonder Jerry stepped off a lake-crossing
Ferry in Michigan and never left, man
Of gumption and sudden tears--he endured much

With dignity. I touched his head again
An hour after his death on a February morning,
My hand carrying the cool imprint
Of low hills through the long drive home.

FROM THE AIRLINER HYMNAL

I steadied the arm of the old man
Who wobbled on the jetway. Now
In mid-flight he drags one foot after
The other up the aisle, reaching out
To seatbacks for balance, his shaky
Hands afflicted with Parkinson's,
As were my mother's.
                           At her funeral,
I listened to organ music with my
Murmuring sisters, remembered
How even in her twenties
My mother's lips moved during Mass
In a faint whisper. She inclined faithfully
Toward the infinite all her life—
It seemed, at the last, to lean
With her, a presence in the sickroom,
Separate yet enveloping her body
And ours, sons and daughters,
And the chair, the adjustable bed,
A rosary, small statues of St. Therese
And the Virgin, tubes and the quietly
Humming machines.

                    I turn my
Grey head to the airplane window,
Peer at the darkness beyond my reflection,
And below, a lit-up city passing away.
I look at the backs of my hands,
Liver spots on loosening skin, and listen
To coughs and soft snores, the old man
Humming to himself as he
Shuffles along, and for a moment I wish
We'd all awake and burst into song,
Sing about speed and stillness

And the feeling of being suspended
Between earth and heaven, sing
Him back until he settles, secure
Again among his fellow passengers.

ABSENCES

Nightjars glide, then white wingbars speed up—
They feed on gnats, flies, mosquitoes, invisible

Down here at dusk, warm for late September,
Yellow leaves scattered over lawns and sidewalks.

Someone's playing a piano, a tune
That catches me off guard. Tears

Almost come—there's the aftertaste
Of a childhood memory, but no room

Or home, no familiar field or street,
Only this space where the rest of my body

Might be, and moths, a porch light,
A man shaking out the pages

Of his newspaper, and the name of that
Song on the tip of my tongue.

PART 6 LISTENING

REQUEST

I want each word of this poem
To listen, as if leaning out
From a windowsill in a small town
When church bells reverberate
Among high bluffs that slope down
To a harbor in summer. I want

The organs and nerves and bones
Of this poem to vibrate, attuned
To the waves, the layers of sound,
To listen right down to the foundations
Of the church, the houses, to listen
Beneath the breakers, the docks, the trout

And the perch, beneath childhood,
The whispers and shouts of
Hide and seek, to listen
Even deeper, down where
Silence begins, where its giver,
Needing nothing, gives and gives.

HIDE AND SEEK

Our bicycle wheels rolled like
Orbiting worlds, moving through time
To God knows where as we pedaled
Hard out of town into the beckoning
Countryside. In the evening,
Behind the oleanders, deep
In the sumac, in crawlspaces
And a cardboard carton leaning
Against a shed, we hunkered down,
Trembling with secrets. Cindy
And Karen, Wardie, Richie, everyone
From our block breathing quietly
Or holding it in, excited
To bursting, barely aware
Of Venus and the first stars
And the full moon, big on the rim
Of the harbor, its yellow rising—
How imperceptibly it climbed,
Slowly, slowly changing color
Through the count and
The ready-or-not and the running
Seeker, who hollered "Here I come!"
Into the tensed, tall, secret silence
Which held us all.

ROUGH CIRCLES

A bird in a fir tree, and beyond
The bird a mountain range
Makes a rough circle around

The sprawling city, Oaxaca,
Where the bird lifts toward
Cirrus clouds, cumulus, no

Shape ever quite the same.
Last night a half-hidden moon,
A reminder to some Zapotecs

Of the year's thirteen cycles
And the ways the invisible
Permeates the visible, of

History and the gods who replace
Gods endlessly. Below
The darkened blue dome

Of sky, the shredded
Clouds, the nimbus
Of the moon, it took us

Five full minutes to circle
The tree of Tule, its trunk wide
And deep as a hacienda.

Two-thousand or more years old,
The Tule's living roots reach
Under the church Franciscans built

To sanctify it, down
Under Our Lady of Solitude, her
Dress like a black pyramid, under

Painful wooden kneelers,
The rose-covered altar, the faithful
Who cross themselves with holy water,

Under the pigeons, the swallows
Circulating in the eaves, the bell tower,
The bell ringing in the hour.

SKY PRAISES

Bubbling oatmeal starts to thicken
    while toast pops up. The spinning
planet seems to quicken--
    a cloudy Sunday's beginning

with layered masses of gray,
    slow-moving, wind-aided,
and now and then one swift ray
    of sunlight, newly created,

it seems, then dispelled
    again. The blooming redbud tree
darkens, as if about to be felled,
    and the radio preacher says we

must worship in the name of Jesus
    because Jesus died for us. I ponder
the logic of that, pause
    before I twist the dial, wonder

how the power of a holy name
    works, exactly, all this repetition
of Allah, Krishna, Rama--
    maybe we partition

the mind, keep it away
    for awhile from the humdrum
blather of thought, the everyday,
    give it something to come

home to. But names pass like light
    and shadow across the ceiling of the mind,
deceiving, revealing, dark, bright,
    though we try to find

what we feel, and a language for it.
    Today I'll raise
the roof a little, walk out
    into the slow-arriving season, praise

the fitful sun, the shapely clouds,
    bring the kids, send up the kites.
I like to hear their shouts,
    faces lifted toward those heights.

THE JUGGLER'S HEART

Something like a sea-pump
With valves and vena cavas,
It keeps the balls in the air,
Juices veins and arteries
For hands, arms, insteps
That obey, after long
And arduous practice,
The brain's commands:
Catch lightly, shift, toss—

On a good night, sitting
In the front row, you might
Hear what you see:
An elliptical hum,
The high pitch of a near
Perfect oval, low thrum
Of the orbits, reminders
Of that music the spheres
Make, and the distant ocean.

A LITTLE NIGHT MUSIC

I know your sighs well,
Your breath arguing
With the author, diminuendos
Of dissent that punctuate

Long silences. Time
To close the book on
Exasperation, love,
Put out the light. I'll open

The windows even wider—
We've never had a quarrel
With rippling air after
Kicked-back covers

In summer, nor
With the owl's
One-word call, so
Frugal and agreeable.

ADMISSIONS

Startled by the sudden
Strangeness of that entity
In the hallway mirror
Who moved when I moved,
His eyes more troubled
Than I like to admit,
I reached toward the face
Of my double, watched
His fingertips approach—
I knew his liver spots,
Forehead scars, deepening
Pores, and the all but
Ceaseless prattle of his
Brain-sealed mind-talk,
The interior play-by-play
Man who won't let
The action speak
For itself. This morning,

Though, as I walked
A corridor of pines,
There was a clearing—
I heard the wind and nothing
Else at all, and turned to kiss
The woman I love, fully
Inhabiting, for a graced
Moment, the give and take
Of touch that admits
The utterly familiar other.

SELF ADVICE

Stop treating your list like the Ten
Commandments. The dog will live
Another day without the brand name
Shampoo, you can survive without
Kalamata olives, and your benign boss
Won't fire you because just one document
Fell through the cracks. Go ahead,
Buy the winter jacket—item 6—
But wear it while you learn
To court the wind's inefficient

Sense of direction, the way
It plays among the pines, rattles
Windows and drainpipes—
These sounds are grace notes
To memory, not reproofs
For lost time, nor even messages
From childhood, but merciful
Suggestions to be still for as long
As it takes, to stand with open palms
In an attitude of listening.

TO BLESSED MARY

The faithful call you Ever Virgin
For your spaciousness,
Hands that refuse nothing,
Cradling the luminous infant
And the death's head. Your eyes,
The blue folds of your gown
Welcome my mother's secrets.
In my dream last night,
She was no older than twenty,
Her skin like yours
In a painting by Raphael,
But she's borne ten children,
And our grown-up needs
And dreams devise many versions
Of her. In mine, you both
In your own ways know
The spirit of clarity
And all the confusion
Of incarnation. Now
My mother walks a narrow
Desert path at the base
Of California mountains, listens
For coyotes, mourning doves,
The many-voiced mockingbird,
The mountains tapering down
To silence. Often her fingers
Tell the mysteries of your
Rosary, and her whispered
Prayers remember each of us,
Bead by bead by bead.

DOUBLE EXCAVATION

In this body now, molecules
Slough off a million at a crack,
Memories seep irretrievably
Into neuronal strata, and ideas
Dry up, drift away like snakeskin
From windswept rock.
                        April's first
Attic kisses, a Peruvian summer,
Last week's tipsy night out with friends
Seem as long gone as those ancient
Inventors of the waxrigger, the emblem,
And the nostrumeme.
                         Same old story—
Civilizations collapsing slowly from within,
Or quickly when superior armor flashed
In sunlight on the hills above the city,
Or avalanches after earthquakes
Hurried them into the sea.
                            Post-catastrophe
Ulnas and tibias, striated skulls,
The hard-working brains of archaeologists
Trying to get a fix on the dead,
While I keep excavating the temple
Floor of my own interior, try
To reconstruct this scattering
Of fragments and shards, but the body's
Subatomic particles whirl ceaselessly,
And the mind never stops quivering
With thought, looking for a pattern
Born of the living stillness that might be
The source of all these questions and motions.

TIME OUT OF TIME

Time is always offering up
A version of itself, Newtonian,
Say, the endless cycles of the Hindus
And Mayans, or Einstein's bends
And loops. Mostly time feels

More solid than my refrigerator,
Bigger than a Great Lake
Or the Rockies, faster than a speeding
Death-dealing bullet you either ride on
Or race ahead of, so just shoot me

If my only choices are saddling up
Or being chased. I sit and breathe
In and out, my particular life stretched
Behind and rippling into the future,
And once in a great while I hear

A faint background hum, maybe
The Om of eternity from which time
Sprouts, flourishes, dies,
Knowable only in that hum
Or a flash, a time out of time,

Then gone, gone like your last
Conversation, gone beyond
The wind-matted, dried-up gardens
Of memory, then, who knows,
Bending, looping back.

ABOUT THE AUTHOR

Skip Renker has degrees from Notre Dame and Duke and an MFA from Seattle Pacific University. His poems have appeared in *California Quarterly*, *Poetry Midwest*, *Small Brushes*, *Spirit First*, and numerous other publications, as well as the *Atlanta Review*, *Passages North*, and *Allegheny River* anthologies. He's published a chapbook, *Birds of Passage* (Delta Press), and *Sifting the Visible* (Mayapple Press), and he conducts workshops and college classes in meditation, world religions, and writing. Skip is the father of two grown children, grandfather of three, and lives with his wife Julia Fogarty in Midland, Michigan.

ACKNOWLEDGEMENTS

These poems appeared in the following publications, sometimes in altered form and under different titles.

Allegheny River, "I Bow to the River"
Atlanta Review, "Your Money"
California Quarterly, "Anesthesia"
Controlled Burn, "A Garbage Sutra," "Self-Advice," "Shoes Outside a Door," "Temple Directive"
Creative 360, "A Momentary Obedience"
kaleidowhirl, "A Friendly Geometry," "The Heart Patient's Instructions," "A Peter Lorre Biopic"
Leelanau Historical Museum, "On Sleeping Bear Dunes"
Paradidomi Review, "From a Raised Chair," "To Blessed Mary"
Passager, "Admissions"
Poetry Midwest, "Sky Praises"
Poetry Super Highway, "Great Aunt Gertrude's First Wedding"
Small Brushes, "A Grave Man," "In the Feel"
Spirit First, "A Silent Reach"
Temenos, "Owing the Light," "Truth and a French Red"
Triplopia, "A Cormorant's Grip," "Rough Circles"
Windfall, "Snout"

Birds of Passage, Delta Press, "Snout" (chapbook)
Sifting the Visible, Mayapple Press, "Absences," "The Appetites"

Anthologies

Allegheny River Anthology, "I Bow to the River"
Atlanta Review Ten Year Anniversary, "Your Money"
Passager Anthology, "Admissions"

Some of these poems won or placed in various competitions; "A Grave Man" received a Pushcart Prize nomination.

FURTHER ACKNOWLEDGEMENTS

I'm grateful to these people for their help in bringing this book about. Ron Starbuck, for his support and astute editorial guidance, Francine Sterle for her generous, careful reading of an earlier version, and Jean Connor for her continuing presence in my life and approach to writing. I'd also like to thank Alex Coldwell, Helen Ruggieri, Ron Ellis, Larry and Cheryl Levy, Laurene Burns, Paula, Chris, and Corey Renker, and many other people – including the wonderful staff at Desert House of Prayer. Forgive me if I did not include your name here! Thanks also to the late William Stafford, Dorothy Stafford, and Emma Lou Thayne.

CPSIA information can be obtained
at www.ICGtesting.com
Printed in the USA
FSOW01n0452210417
33350FS

9 780998 640426